An ABC of DEMOCRACY

Nancy Shapiro   Paulina Morgan

Frances Lincoln
Children's Books

Dear growing one, when you were born you couldn't say anything, and your caregivers had to figure out everything you needed. As a baby, you couldn't make choices for yourself but now you can make so many. You might decide what you will play, or which book you will read, or even what help you might give to someone else.

As you grow, you will make more and more decisions. That's one of the best parts of growing up! It's a big responsibility to make decisions that are good for you while considering others.

You may have noticed that in lots of places, certain people are in charge, and sometimes you have choices and other times you are told what you must do. Homes, schools, towns, and countries all have rules and people in charge. Democracy is a way of governing where everyone has a say in who will lead and what decisions and rules will be made.

Over time you will have more of a voice in many communities. You will have the power to stand up for what you believe in and maybe even run for public office. As you make your way through this world, perhaps you will discover something you really care about, like protecting the environment or making sure that you and your friends are all treated fairly — you can use your voice to help make a difference.

It's important to discover what you care about— open your eyes to the world and know that your presence can help make a difference. It's your right to know that you are free to try to make change, and to vote in every election as soon as you are old enough. Learn, play, explore, and be curious about our amazing world because this is just the beginning!

Here's to your growing voice!

Nancy Shapiro

Make a difference by e-mailing and writing letters to leaders, or protesting to make your voice heard. Join other activists to make a change for what you believe in.

is for ACTIVISM

Speak up for someone or anything
you care about!

When voting, you mark a paper ballot, or sometimes use a voting machine. You might be choosing a person to be in charge or saying "yes" or "no" to a question. The ballots are counted and the most votes wins.

is for BALLOTS

A way to cast your vote in secret.

About half the world lives in democratic countries where the citizens have the power to vote. The other half lives in authoritarian countries where the people in charge have all the power.

is for COUNTRY

A nation run by its own government.

Democracy is one type of government. Citizens get to elect their leaders and have more say in how the government is run. What decisions would you like to have a say in where you live?

is for DEMOCRACY

How are decisions made where you live?

The more you know, the more power you will have to make good choices. Reading, going to classes, and being interested in your community will help you be informed.

is for EDUCATE

Stay informed.

Freedom means everyone being able to practice their own religion, share thoughts, like and love who they want, and live unique lives. In a free society, as long as our actions don't harm others, we all have the freedom to be ourselves without getting into trouble.

is for FREEDOM

The power to think and do what you want.

Governments are responsible for towns, cities, and countries. They make laws, follow rules, and exist to represent and take care of their people. Are there rules where you live? What would happen if there weren't any?

is for GOVERNMENT

An elected group of people in charge.

Everyone is born with human rights and those should be protected forever. Some of these rights are: to be safe, to believe whatever you choose, and to be free.

is for HUMAN RIGHTS

Human rights—everyone has them.

In a democracy, everyone should be represented
when governments make decisions. Be curious about
different opinions and backgrounds and try to help
those with quieter voices be heard.

is for INCLUSIVE

You belong; no one should be left out.

Justice is everyone behaving fairly toward each other. The justice system is made up of police, courts, and judges. It is supposed to make sure people follow rules and are safe, while treating them with respect.

is for JUSTICE

Justice for all.

You can canvass your neighbors to help someone get elected. Tell them about the candidate, the person you hope gets elected, and what makes them special. Spread the word and let them know when and where to vote!

is for KNOCK ON DOORS

Knock on neighbors' doors and discuss your views.

Democracy should be ruled by laws and everybody has to follow them. No matter what your job is, even if you work for the government, you have to follow the law.

is for RULE OF LAW

Fairness matters—everyone should follow the same rules.

If the majority group wants to play tag, then tag it is! However, the smaller minority group, who wanted to watch videos, should still be treated just as nicely. These are called minority and majority rights.

is for MINORITY AND MAJORITY RIGHTS

Minority or majority—you still have the same rights.

Democracy means "people rule." This means that it can't be just one person making decisions. Every citizen needs to help and vote to make a difference.

is for NEED

Democracy needs everyone's participation
to run at its best.

People working in a public office are expected
to serve the public and do their job with
responsibility and honesty.

is for OFFICE

Public office is a job in the government.

If you were a politician, you could suggest, create, and support rules and solutions to help everyone! The public would be putting their trust in you.

is for POLITICIAN

Politicians are people elected to work in government.

You can help the government to serve people best by asking questions. If someone representing you makes a choice you are curious about, ask them a question!

is for QUESTIONS

Go ahead and ask!

When we elect someone, we are choosing them to make the right decisions on our behalf. You would be representing your friends if they chose you to decide what kind of game you should all play.

is for REPRESENTATION

When one person makes choices for many others.

In many democratic countries, some groups of people, such as women, haven't always had the right to vote. Over time, suffrage movements and activists have helped get more people that right.

is for SUFFRAGE

The right to vote.

You may not be old enough to vote yet, but you can still make a difference. Turn Up at protests, tell others about elections, spread the word about how we can all help make a change, and encourage everyone to vote.

CLIMATE

is for TURN UP

Be counted!

Democracy is designed so that everyone has
the power to rise up. Everyone (you too!) can
help uplift people who need support.

is for UPLIFTING

Lifting people up is valued.

vote

Voting is what you do when you cast your ballot. You might be choosing who you want to be leader or deciding what you think about a question. When people ask, "Who are you voting for?", it means an election and the chance to vote is coming!

is for VOTING

Voting is a central part of the democratic process.

Elections are a way to vote and can be used for lots of different things. To win an election politicians need the most votes. They work to become known by the public and persuade people to vote for them.

is for WINNING

Winning is how politicians get into office.

The government has many parts that work together.
The Legislative Branch makes the laws while the
Executive Branch carries them out. The system is
like a bicycle. It has wheels, pedals, and handlebars
that all work together to help you go places.

is for EXECUTIVE BRANCH

One of the many parts of government.

Speak up! Democracy is an inclusive political system. Your voice is supposed to be heard. Everyone should feel welcome to speak their minds about anything.

is for YOUR VOICE

Your voice is key in a democracy!

People born in a specific country or have a parent who is a citizen there, usually are automatically citizens of that place. Citizens make a difference—learn about what is happening in your community, protest, vote, and maybe even run for public office someday.

free

is for CITIZEN

Legal residents of a country who can use their energy and enthusiasm to keep democracy strong.

Nancy Shapiro helped create the non-profit organization, TurnUp Activism. She runs their training program whose mission is to promote youth voter turnout and activism. She is a clinical psychologist in private practice and performs and teaches the oboe. She is a mother of three, plays tennis, composes music, cycles, and reads.

Paulina Morgan works as an independent illustrator based in Santiago de Chile. She studied design before moving to Barcelona, Spain, to obtain her master's degree in Art Direction. She worked in advertising before deciding to pursue her passion for illustration.

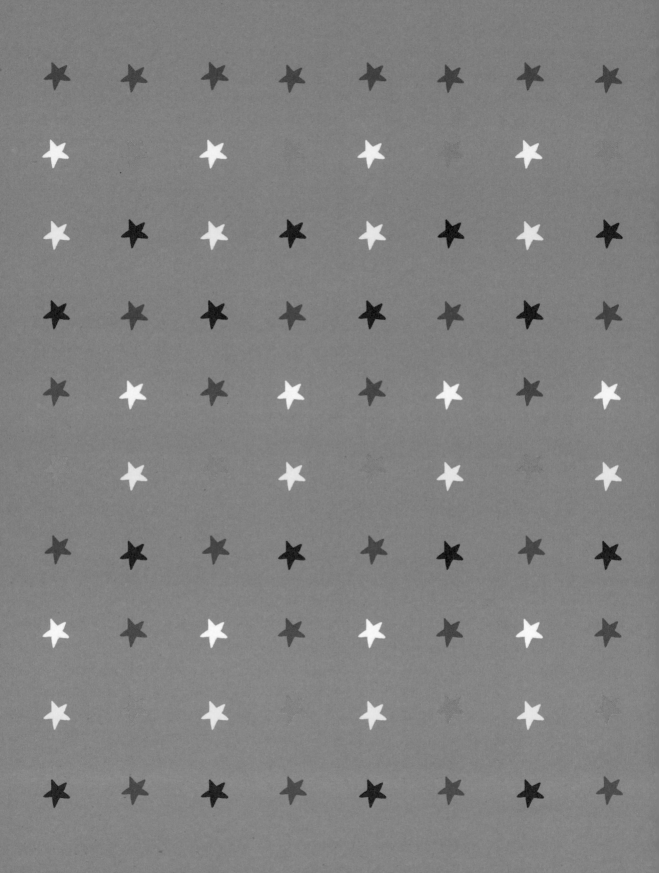